MOM!

Parent~
Oetry

Illustrated &
Written by
ATK

T
W H

Amazon Kindle Direct Publishing

https://kdp.amazon.com

Copyright © 2020 ATK

Trigger warning:

These poems I wrote have a strong sense of sarcasm, can make fun of situations that are not all that funny with a dark sense of humor and may trigger some strong emotional responses. Some poems are heart felt, some are not. Some show the struggles of parenting.

In addition, because I am mother, I have written any version of the word "Mom" in the lines, but Dad could easily replace Mom. I know some dads that have this thing called parenting better than I!

At the end of the day, we are all in this together, parenting is hard, children are hard, this world is hard. Sometimes we need to vent and other times we need support. Just know that when you are reading this, you are not alone in your parenting journey.

Also, minor crude language warning!

Table of Contents:

PART ONE:

PART TWO:

PART 1:

The "Funny"
Struggles of
Parenting

Sweetest Child of Mine

Oh, sweetest child of mine

I will love you until the end of
time

Do you want some cheese with
that whine?

Are you really making me ask a
second time?

Don't you cross that line

Shh, now Mommy needs that glass
of wine.

POOP

What's something you'd never
thought would be the hottest
topic of conversation?

POOP

What will make you want to
whine?

POOP

What did you just talk about at
dinner time?

POOP

What's that smell?

POOP

What makes that diaper swell?

POOP

What's that on your clothes?

POOP

What was just squashed between
your toes?

POOP

What is something you may fight
about?

POOP

What will make you want to
shout?

POOP

What will make you celebrate?

POOP

What will make you *ULTRA* late?

POOP

What is that art upon the wall?

POOP

What is our favorite word of
all?

POOP

It's Time to GO!

It's 6:50, it's time to go

I have calmly asked you to put
on your shoes

But that's not what you choose

It's 6:55, it's still time to go

I have brought you your shoes

Please put them on

But you grab your Nerf gun and
scream GAME ON!

It's 7:00 and my patience is
dwindling

And now, we are wrestling

It's 7:05

SHOES ARE ON!

It's time to get in the car

The ride isn't all that far

I internally cheer as we are
somewhat on time

I grab the keys

And what to I turn around to
see?

You're full blown nakey standing
there

Smiling at me because….

Your shoes are on

P.A.R.E.N.T.I.N.G

P is for proud, patience,
problematic and pain

A is for artful, arguing,
anxiety and action

R is for relentless, ruthless,
reckless and reassurance

E is for evolving, enthusiasm,
exhaustion and exciting

N is for nudity, negotiating,
never-ending and nice

T is for terrifying, taunting,
thrilling and triumph

I is for incredible, illogical,
intensified, and important

N is for natural, nauseating,
naïve and needed

G if for gory, grand, gratifying
and glorified

Parenting Haiku 1

Can I? Can I? Please

No way, you cannot do that

Why you ask? Because!

Don't Fight!

Please don't fight

You do this to your sister day
and night

Do not undermine your brother's
might

This will not be a fair fight

Please don't make me wash blood
out of white

Why don't you just go play
or fly a kite

That would be a better
sight

No, okay, you want to give
your mother a fright

Okay, cool, it is time
for bed

GOOD NIGHT!

13

I'm Raising Gremlins

Children are funny
Not one is the same as the other
Children are crazy
I swear it's not from their
mother

Children are wonderful
They are innocent and pure
But there's somethings I've
learned

And that's for damn sure
Don't feed them after midnight
Even if it's only this once
Your bed will be covered in it
and to clean it will take months

Do not get them wet
They turn into ravenous beasts
Especially if washing their hair
at the least

Children are lovely and all
kinds of emotions

Proceed with caution

The gremlins,

I mean children,

Know that loving them

Is like riding the waves of the
ocean

Parenting Haiku 2

Don't touch your sister

Is what I say all darn day

But it doesn't work

Repeat After Me

Repeat after me
Well, now that I say this, don't
I often scream
To ensure that I don't crack at
the seam

I get frustrated
And probably look constipated
I have the mouth of a sailor
And will swear without failure
I always hope no kid is near
But they ALWAYS hear
They are sneaky about it
Until they drop something
And yell S@#T
Palm to the face
We have got to get out of this
space

Do not repeat after your mother
(But there'll always be another)

Brush, Brush, Brush

When I was younger, I loved
practicing doing hair

I would brush and style my dolls
and mother

(she is a saint)

I was happy when my daughter's
hair got so long

I was excited for all the styles
we could try

But boy, was not prepared for
this marathon

We picked out the brush

We picked out the bows

We picked out the detangling
spray that smells like a rose

We picked out our spot to sit

I make the first pass with the
brush

And think to myself, that this
is a breeze

I make the second pass
It's wiggle, wiggle freeze
I make the third pass
And now she's off running
Fourth pass
Her look will no longer be
stunning

Fifth pass
She's starting to scream
Sixth pass
Now I'm starting to scream
Seventh pass
We are almost done with this
section of hair

Eighth pass
Forget the bow, I don't care
Nineth pass

We are in this to win this
despite all the fretting

Tenth pass

Why am I sweating?

Eleventh pass

We've reached silent tears

Twelfth pass

We are done with over
enthusiastic cheers

<u>Parenting Haiku 3</u>

Children are so gross

They pick and eat their boogers

Like it is their job

C.H.I.L.D.R.E.N

C is for crazy, chaos, crusty,
clumsy, and cool

H is for hectic, helpful,
healing, hellions and hearts

I is for irritable, intense,
imagination and icky

L is for love, light, late and
lively

D is for daunting, delightful,
deafening and dreamy

R is for remembering, realistic,
ruthless and rare

E is for elegant, emotional,
everything and everlasting
(love)

N is for nakedness, neat, noble
and nifty

Kid Art

Kids are creative

Kids are imaginative

They work hard on their art

They want to touch your heart

They've worked all day

With crayons, paint, markers and
clay

There is glitter everywhere

That'll never go away I swear

Its been hours of work

Now they're getting a fork.

You wait patiently

While they work diligently

You see them take out the paint
brush

You don't want them to feel
rushed

But you're sure the clay has
turned to mush

Now smooshed into your carpet

You think to yourself just drop
it

Finally, they're done

You can't wait to see

The paper they bring is droopy

The paint hasn't dried

Your carpet has now died

You plaster a smile on your face

As you see the mess in this
space

They hand you the paper to look

It has the weight of a book

You look down and stare

Careful to show you care

Your child's face lights up

Their eyes like a pup

You turn the paper to the side

In hopes to not hurt their pride

You guess what it is

But that never works

It's a goopy mess by now

Yet somehow

This is the greatest thing you

have ever seen

Parenting Haiku 4

Why am I so wet?

Why do your pants look like
that?

Oh, the diaper exploded

Can I do that Please Mommy?

"Can I do that pleeeeasee?" Is
what you ask

No, you cannot body slam your
sister from the couch

No, you cannot stick your hand
in the hole in the bottom of the

Toilet and touch

No, you cannot ride your
skateboard down the roof

No, you cannot eat cake for
breakfast even if you brush your
one tooth

No, you cannot just poop in the
yard like the dog

No, you cannot shoot nerf darts
out your bedroom window while
people jog

No, you cannot use the jump rope
to rappel

No, you cannot make a bike train
with your sister and bell

No, you cannot fly like a bird
No, you cannot ride on the roof
of the car, you turd

You ask why
I give you a million reasons why
You ask why again

I say with much chagrin

BECAUSE I SAID SO!

And now you have made me sound

like my mother you know?

Parenting Haiku 5

You have cried all night

I just want to sleep right now

Now I am crying

You Say, I say

You say good morning

I say, five more minutes of
sleep please

You say "uh oh"

I say "oh no"

You say right now

I say one minute please

You say more

I say not right now

You say let's play

I say okay

You say Mama

I say I love you

You say poop

I say let's change your butt

You say s@%t

I say we don't use that word

Just One More Minute Please

You have fought me for more than
2 hours

It's time to go to bed

We've gotten 18 cups of water
that you have requested

And for poison they have been
tested

We've checked under your bed and
in your closet

Stories are read even though you
try to pause it

You are tucked in tight, with
your left foot out

Your stuffy is in your arms, but
you still shout

We sing song number 20

I kiss you goodnight a plenty

I walk out of your room and turn
out the light

From down the hall I can hear
the sniffles

I beg for one more minute of
quiet

I count the seconds in my head
The sniffles get louder and the
crying starts from your bed

I think to myself they will calm
down in one more minute

I wait patiently hoping, holding
my breath to not jinx it

I hope they do not sense my
hesitation

The cries are louder, my
hesitation was sensed

I walk into your room; the tears
stop, a smile has spread

I think to myself

They've got me good I said

33

I repeat the process another
three times

I walk out of the room for one
last time

It's late now and I'm tired

I go to bed

I've spent the night being woken
up several times

You crawl out of your bed and
sneak into my room

Just before the morning sun

You jump on me and say it's time
to play

I beg, just one more minute
please

Parenting Haiku 6

Splash, splash in the tub

Water, water everywhere

Bubbles, toot, oh poop

Wakey, Wakey Eggs and Bacy
(Bacon)

Wakey, wakey rise and shine

It's time to start our daily
grind

The sun's not up

But you don't care

You're excited to play
downstairs

I slowly grumble as I get up

Stretch, stretch, pop, pop

Your brother and sister are
already downstairs

Begging for a special breakfast

I find my PJ pants strewn out on
the floor

You kindly threw them there
during the night before

I throw up my hair that's an
entangled mess

Oof, what's that smell

Oh, it's just that diaper with
that enormous swell

We change your diaper

We get down the steps

I rush to get breakfast done
before there's any upsets

Eggs are made

This happens every 6 months

We all sit to eat before the
daily rush

I smile and inhale my food
before it turns to mush

I look to see who's still eating

And low and behold

It's the dog who's been eating
off your fork

I guess you don't like eggs
anymore

Tinkle, Tinkle Little Star

Tinkle, Tinkle my little star

How I wonder where you are

Up at the top of the stairs so

high

I can see it coming straight for

my eyes

Tinkle, Tinkle my little star

How I wonder where your diapers

are

It Takes Two

Oh, look it's a new baby

Mommy, Daddy and Baby make three

These early days a tough

They are filled with so much
stuff

Mommy stays home while on leave

Daddy gets to work, oh that
peeve

Mommy pouts

While Daddy is out

When Mommy gets a break

The Baby never stays awake!

When Daddy stays home

The outsiders roam

They "ooh" and they "ahh"

Thinking Mommy has gone to the
spa

They think Daddy babysat

Um, hello? No. Let's have a chat

It takes two you see

To make this baby

We do not "babysit"

We both deal with this s#@t

We trade off at night

We deal with the fight

We are a team

However, it's not always a dream

So, when you see one of us out

Do not shout

Let us enjoy our time

Before we go home to be

covered in little

kid slime

PART 2:

Poems with Love and Emotion

It's My Party

Oh, the day has come where you
are turning one!

We've spent weeks planning for
the fun

The balloons, the cake, the
favors, the guests

We have done our absolute best
We decorate like crazy and bust
our butts

We try so hard to make the
picture-perfect day

We internally scream and cry and
pray

The love is there
Chaos fills the air
Time flies and the party is
almost done

We can't forget to sing your
song

Your face is filled with a smile
Our faces smile as we sing
Our hearts swell and eyes start
to sting

We can't believe how fast you've
grown

And all the new things that are
left to be shown

The candles are out
You start to pout
We give you the cake
Oh, the messy face you make
To cute to care about the mess
We just know that we are

blessed.

What A Mess

Managing a family, work and
house is a daunting task

There's laundry, toys, crumbs
and floors to be mopped

There's food to be made and
groceries to be got

There are things that grow mold,
become mildewy and gross

You're not sure of the last time
the dog got a bath

There are drawings on the wall
and cracks in the tile

The toilet is missed, tile is
now stained yellow

There is task after task, you
never stop going

The tears will be flowing
without anyone knowing

You say to yourself that I will
get this tomorrow

But it will sit on the floor for
a week or four

The bustle of life keeps you
going day and night

You sleep for a few, but the
mind does not rest

You think to yourself what a
mess this place is

But when you take a step back a
see this mess means more

It means your children have
clothes, toys and food

Your children are happy, and
you'll get really sappy

They'll never go hungry through
bellies or mind

You foster their knowledge and
help them grow over time

The memories are made and will
eventually be missed

Moments go by as fast as a
toddler's kiss

You know what will always be
there, the mess

You know what won't always be
there, the children

So, for now that pile of clothes
in the corner can sit

The toys strewn about can wait
for a day

The mildew and dust are not just
a must

For what a mess means nothing
now

Not more than your memories,
moments or love

So, go on a play, cleaning can
come another day

Parenting Haiku 7

I push, grunt and scream

I think I can't do this thing

But baby's snuggled tight

No One Told Me

No one told me that becoming a
mom was going to be…

The hardest job on the planet

The role is always shape
shifting

Your body is always changing

The post-partum days are
mystifying

The days are short

The nights are long

You'll leak from everywhere

It's okay to cry

It's okay to step away

You cook meals that no one will
eat

You'll always talk about poop

Your meal is usually always cold

And you'll never pee alone

You may only live in PJs on your
days home

No one is perfect

No one is the same

That this is the most rewarding
job

That everything will work itself
out

That it is okay to ask for help

No one told me that my heart
could grow and that these
children will always make it so.

Goodnight, Sleep Tight

Bedtime is the least favorite
part of the day

Or at least that's what they say

Maybe bedtime isn't for the kids

Even though, we know it really
is

Let's pretend for one minute
that the kids' bedtime,

It's for us

The kids fight the whole time

And boy do they whine

But once they settle it's a
whole new world

The stories you read help grow
their imagination

The songs you may sing, do
wonders for them

The snuggles you give, heal you
both

The hugs and the kisses will
make you smile

And as you walk out of the room
You find that the day was tough
Did you do enough?
Self-doubt sinks in
You fret over all the things
that were missed

As the world of anxieties hit
you

Know that your children don't
see this

There little heads are resting
(eventually) on their pillows

Their heads are filled with
dreams of smiles, hugs and fun

They are waiting for the rise of
the morning sun

They are happy, healthy and fed

You go in one last time to kiss
their head

Don't worry so

Tomorrow you'll give it another
go

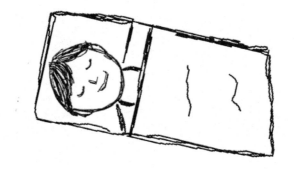

Parenting Haiku 8

Sleeping through the night

Are we sure that she's alright?

Get up, check and see

This "ish" is HARD

Parenting is hard

That is the understatement of
the year

There is so many judgements
passed

Days filled with fear

Days filled with tears

Days filled with anxieties

Days filled with nothing but the
bare necessities

You may find yourself always
second guessing

There's no instruction manual
for this

The world is ever changing

The trends and the expectations

This, weighs heavy on the heart

However, parenting isn't a
refined art

It's more of like a defensive
game

Running strategies to protect
our children

The world is scary
Hearts fill with worry
These days won't last forever
Or so we are always told
We will miss this when we are
old

My hopes in life
While we go through this strife
Is to rise above it all
Even if I fall
Remember you've got this
No matter what happens
Take it second by second
There's no winning
This isn't a race
This is a journey

To provide your kids with grace

We've got this notion

We're filled with emotion

We are stronger than before

Smile, deep breaths

You've got this mama

You are the best

Postpartum is a Beast

The flood of emotions after
delivery is insane

There's no wonder there's a
rollercoaster in our brain

The post-delivery exhaustion
doesn't compare

To the following days that can
cause great despair

Everyone is happy to see your
new bundle of joy

Yet your heart feels like a toy

Sleepless nights, zombie days
Boobs are leaking, pressure
builds up and they spray

You weren't expecting that
But what's more the baby spat
You're tired, you're sore, you
can't wash your hair

The simplest of tasks become
frightening and such a nightmare

You sink into silence, thinking
what's wrong

You're thinking that this isn't
where you belong

I can't say don't worry
Because the depression becomes
blurry

But what I can say
Is seeking help is okay
You weren't meant to do this
alone

That New Baby Smell

When I was young, I never
understood why mothers smelled
the

Heads of new babies

They always said there's that
new baby smell

I thought they were crazy as all
hell

Since most babies smell like
spit up or sour milk

Well that changed over time

I had my own

And now that they are grown

I miss the scent of that new
baby smell

Parenting Haiku 9

Giggling child

The best sound that's ever heard

Let's keep that smile

First Day Jitters

We spent the first 4 years of
your life together

We had a routine
We played and we learned
We laughed and we cried
We talked about how big you have
gotten

The past week had flown by
We went shopping for school
supplies

You picked out your new backpack
(rainbow unicorn of course)

We picked out your lunch box
with matching thermos

We picked out your first day
outfit

We spent extra time snuggling
the night before

We sang and read stories galore

We sprinkled your first day
jitters sparkles and tucked you
in tight

You got lots of hugs and kisses
goodnight

The morning came fast
I promised those jitters
wouldn't last

It was a family affair, but I
wasn't prepared

We walked to the school
You had a brave smile on your
face

You were so excited to start
this new adventure

I watched you walk into the
building with a smile on my face

My heart was full of pride

Yet I cried

It wasn't long until the day was
over

We picked you up

And the jitters were done

You talked and had lots of fun

And couldn't wait for the next
morning sun

Laundry, Laundry Everywhere

Laundry, laundry everywhere

Why do I even care?

It's wash, fold, dry and put
away

It's a job that's done everyday

I swear the children have more
stuff than I

There's no way to catch up, why
do I try?

Oh, the mountain piles

But I can look and see the
smiles

Those grass stains on the pants?

Those were from a victory dance

That red paint on the shirt?

Valentine's cards and an
accidental squirt

The milk spilt on that pillow

Is from our picnic under the
willow

Laundry may be everywhere, my
friend

But the memories made
Are worth it 'til the end

Happy Tears

Your child says something to
melt your heart

Happy tears and you fall apart

You watch Mickey Mouse Club
House and Donald shares

Those happy tears show you care

You donate all those old baby
clothes

Happy tears and runny nose

Your child asks you snuggle more

Happy tears straight from your
core

You watched some Pixar move with
your kids

You can't hide those happy tears
behind your lids

Your kid says "I love you more"

Happy tears forevermore

Forever and Always

I will love you forever and
always

There is not one thing that
could change that

I will love you forever and
always

Through your smiles, your
cheers, your sadness, your tears

I will love you forever and
always

Through the tantrums, the
screaming, the nightmares and
fears

I will love you forever and
always

Through the sleepless nights and
long, long days

I will love you forever and
always

forever
3
always

Parent Time Out

As a kid I hated time outs

I would sit on the couch and
pout

One time I got smart and hid a
toy in the cushion

Knowing I'd get a time out at
some point

I've put my kids in countless
time outs

To save their sanity

To help with their emotions

To help their siblings
understand we need to use their
words

Not their impulsive reaction

They hated it

We have far less, now that they
are older

But that does not give me a time
to rest

I know this sounds super selfish
We aren't "supposed" to tap out
But mamas and dadas alike
Need a break sometimes
Can we declare parent time outs?
So, we can work through our
emotions

So, we can protect ourselves
So, we can practice our words
and not our reactions

I don't think I would mind a
time out

We are frazzled and frayed
And run ragged all day
Let's discuss
How we go about
A parent time out

Parenting Haiku 10

Kids are like fire

Heartwarming, fierce, fast and
strong

Intense and stunning

Your Worst Nightmare

It's hard to say all your fears
out loud

Try not to stay too proud
It's okay to share
We are never prepared,
For our parenting nightmares
You'll always get stares
As your child freaks out in
public

Your child may get sick
You pray that it is never life
threatening

Your child's screams are always
deafening

You send them to school
Which they think is cool
The teachers are usually great
But that doesn't stop fate

Between bullying, harassment and
shootings galore

You feel like your heart and
brain can't take much more

Your child will tell you some
scary things

All the fears bubble up to the
surface, oh the anxiety it
brings

You must stay strong

To help your child feel that
they belong

But as the go to sleep

You hide and you weep

You reach out for help

But the resources welp

You feel so lost

But you will fight for your
child at any cost

You are literally wearing your
heart on your sleeve

Your sanity that you have lost
will make you grieve

Most days are great
And all worth the wait
Savor the good with every breath
you take

Because all the strife that life
will make

You constantly think
You may need to see a shrink
And this is okay
It's healthier that way
You may feel a bit crass
But remember
This too shall pass

Lessons

On this new journey called
parenting we learn lots of
things
From babies, from friends, from
our own parents
Every day brings a new lesson
A moment for learning
A moment for a blessing
The good and the bad are shared
in every way
The lesson that's taught the
most is who's in your corner
It can't really be learned
unless you hit hard times
You may rely on family or
friends
Be weary of those who cause woe
in the end
Blood isn't always thicker than
water
And friends may not always be
trustworthy

Though the time goes on you
learn who is there
You learn who is a straggler, a
supporter and fretter
You learn fast and hard none the
better
It may be hard to cut off the
"Someone"

Especially where the damage is
done
But it is better for your
survival

Try not to create your archrival
Parenting is hard
Pick those who support you the
most and will stand at guard

No More Babies

The journey begins on one of
your hardest days

All your plans will go up in a
blaze

You push and you scream, the
pain is unreal

But all is forgotten when you
hear that first squeal

You hold your little one tight

You don't want to let them out
of your sight

In the early days, everything is
a mess

Everything is chaos

It's diapers, bottles, outfit
changes and more

Sleepless night after night, not
even one snore

Suddenly, your baby is one

And the party you planned is
done

You watch them grow and point
out their toes

Before you know it, your baby
turns three right under your
nose

You're not sure how this can be,
and time has gone amiss

Those toddler tantrums, you
think won't be missed

Time flies by and your baby
turns five

You spend your last few days
before school starts so alive
Doing all kinds of adventures
from the heart

The first day of school is
exciting and a new start

You hold it together until the
school doors close

And some goo may start to drip
from your nose

It's okay to cry, there won't be
a dry eye

Elementary school goes by fast
as the days are filled, oh my

Your child grows and grows

How much taller no one knows

Then one day it hits you amongst
the chaos

The baby you've had is now lost

There are no more sleepless
nights, cluster feeds, diapers
and screams

There are no more bottles,
binkies, onesies or bad dreams

You remember the time you wished
it were over

The exhaustion usually won,
what's moreover

You continue to tuck your
growing child into bed

You place a kiss on top of their
head

You watch them sleep and
everything's at peace

It's funny to see that
perspective changes everything

The early years of parenting

Are merely survival

Then toddler years are
definitely your rival

Childhood begins,

You watch them grow, become
social and learn with new grins

You hope for the best

But know that your child will
take care of the rest

What I Wish I Could Say

When someone asks you "How are
you?"

As a parent my answer is
generally "good" or "tired"

However, that answer is not
always desired

I'm not sure that any person
wants to know

About my parenting woes

What I wish I could say

Could go on for days

So far now my friends

I will share my favorites that
go along with this parenting
"trend"

I wish I could say

"Not great today"

I wish I could say that

"I slept maybe 15 minutes last
night"

I wish I could say

"I am bloated as heck and my
back is a wreck"

I wish I could say

"I leaked through my clothes and
hid so nobody knows"

I wish I could say

"I cried in the car because my
kids broke my heart"

I wish I could say that

"I want to stay home with my
kids"

But also, when I stay home with
my kids

I wish I could say

"I need a break"

Without being judged

I wish I could say that

"The number of chores or laundry
is daunting"

I wish I could say that

"I don't need a drink I need a
massage"

I wish I could say that

"I just want to sit and binge
watch movies all day"

I wish I could say

"My minds always racing, and sometimes these kids keep me pacing"

I wish I could say

I just need some "alone time"
Without being considered a "bad mom"

There are so many more things

I wish I could say

But that is all for today

TIRED

Every parent is tired

There's no doubt about that

T is for tired, that's obvious
to me

I is for irrational because
that's how we will act
especially if your child is
three

R is for resilient for us
parents, we know how to function
when we are running on empty

E is for exhausted because tired
just isn't enough, you will
learn the true depths of the
exhaustion and be impressed by
the many levels you have
achieved

D is for dazed as you are a
parent with little to no sleep,
you function, you eat, you wash
and repeat, these I call are
your "zombie parent days"

Quarantine

Parenting in quarantine is
everyone's worst nightmare

The entire world is in a great
despair

No one knows quite what to do

And part of your job is
deciphering what's true

First things first

There is tons of hand washing

You stock up on cleaning
supplies

You think you will be okay
you've got enough toilet paper
for days

Then you go to the store for
your normal supply and realize
the world has gone mad as
there's no toilet paper in sight

The shelves look so bare

It gives you a slight scare

You put this aside in your
mental lock box

Second there's schooling, what
the heck do you do about that?

The poor teachers and parents
alike were given no direction

No one plans for a pandemic

Remote learning, we try, but we
all want to die

Then summer comes and all plans
have been ruined

You think to yourself this will
all be over in the fall

But that is not the case at all

School battles begin, do you do
remote or send the children in

What is best, no one knows, but
you'll be judged either way

Third there is the mask, oh the
mask!

It is a wonderful thing as it is
protection for yourself and your
child

You teach your child to wear
the darn mask and keep their
hands to themselves

But don't worry about the mask,
because people will ask, why are
you wearing the mask when you
are out

Then your
child may
see another
person not
wearing a
mask

A tantrum is thrown, and you
wonder how will you do this on
your own

Birthdays are ruined in the
sense there is no friends, no
games, no true physical
interaction

You child will sulk and cause
quite the emotional reaction

You brainstorm all you can and
come up with birthday parades
and online parties

But who are we to expect that
this will fill their need for
other children's' physical
interactions

Lastly, my friends

I don't want to say

The extreme worry and guilt that
you feel everyday

It doesn't seem like it will
ever go away

You worry what if,

What if my child gets sick?

What if I am missing something,
Did I make the right choice

All I can say, though I am no
expert,

I have never parented through a
pandemic before

Is that we are all going through
this

One day at a time

There is no need for hysterics
or gigantic panics

Instead of judging what another
parent does,

We can build each other up

The anxiety we all feel is very, very, real

We are at an internal war with the virus

Because honestly, how dare it even try us

Parents are warriors,

Our children are precious

Let's continue to move forward and grow everyday

Let's continue to raise our future leaders, okay?

We can do this I promise

We have no other choice

Let us remain strong and united with our voice

Because like I have said before

Parenting through this
quarantine is a temporary battle

And nothing more

Innocence

A child has the purest heart in
the world

There is no truer statement that
I have ever told

When your children start to
interact with their world,

And they wander

You realize you get to watch all
this affection and wonder

Their actions are pure

And they are always 100% sure

They are bold and unafraid

Until they may have strayed

When they start to ask questions

You notice their new little
obsessions

And learn about their newest
frustrations

They will do cute things

That will melt your heart

A little hand hold,

A hug or a kiss with make you
fall apart

Watching your child grow

Will never get old

No memory can ever be sold

There will come a day

When your child has learned the
realities of the world,

Or at least so they say

So, hold on tight

And with all your might

And always kiss their head good
night

For one day the innocence will
be gone

And your baby will be grown.

<u>Parenting Haiku 11</u>

Scream, shout pout and more

This is parenting, I'm sure

Love forevermore

Uplifting Days

When becoming a parent

You become good at lots of
things

A caregiver

A lip reader

A doctor

A stylist

And a performer who sings

But the best role you have
adapted too

Will make up for all the poo

Is making your child laugh

They grin and they smile

As you turn into a giraffe

They howl with laughter

If it is the dog, you are
chasing after

They hoot and they holler

As you pretend to be their
caller

They clap and they cheer

While you pretend to disappear

They wiggle and giggle

At the Jell-O you have made
jiggle

The entertainment parenting role

Is always good for your soul

As the days filled with laughter

Are your happy ever after

The End.

About the Author

ATK, is an acronym for Ashley's full name, she is a fulltime mother, full time nurse practitioner and advocate for mental health awareness. She spends her free time writing, helping her children throughout their life and crocheting.

Creating this book of poems over time helped her cope with the stresses of being a mother. These poems were each written with different emotions felt. She wanted to bring normalcy to the struggles of being a parent.